bird of winter

bird of winter

alice hiller

First published 2021 by
Liverpool University Press
4 Cambridge Street
Liverpool
L69 7ZU

British Library Cataloguing-in-Publication data
A British Library CIP record is available

ISBN 978-1-800-34869-1 softback

Typeset by Carnegie Book Production, Lancaster
Printed and bound in Poland by Booksfactory.co.uk

in this place was found
a bronze sistrum

temple of isis pompeii
4 january 1766

o dog of pompeii

your howl was buried under
metres of ash and pumice

torched belly up then cast into stained
plaster from your void of terror

I want to say who bent your neck
how was your arse split

I want to release that studded collar
chained hound of my underworld

o dog of pompeii

you writhe beside forty lucky roman charms
laid out in their glass coffin

taken from the bracelet of the burnt child
found curled on vesuvius's shoreline

whose hunched body carries me back
to the linen sheets and lace counterpane

in my mother's house where the garden
hides dark sheds hung with limp pheasants

where rhododendrons flash
slippery purple pleasures

where the dead eye of the bird bath
looks up   but sees nothing

o dog of pompeii

you turned your head away
while my mother unhooked her corset

and did not dare to growl
or bare your teeth to guard

when I first entered the fish smell
where my mouth tasted wet flesh hair

where I lost you   beloved playmate
as a finger   moved inward

forcing me   whimpering
down warrens   of dark tunnels

o dog of pompeii

here amongst the erotic statues
and carbonised cradles

I find you at last   brought back to me whole
mosaiced to life   and risen again

asking me to throw this red rubber ball
and watch you rush towards it barking

mosaics of guard-dogs have
been found in many houses
in pompeii and herculaneum
reminding guests this was a
protected space

the needle's eye sews red silk

single offence of rape by a single offender
victim under 13   10 years custody

harsh as ash over sunshine

rape accompanied by aggravating factors
victim under 13   13 years custody

pain distils its own weather

repeated rape of same victim by single offender
15 years custody

sometimes death extends a hand

aggravating factors   abuse of trust   sustained attack
background of intimidation or coercion

offers the glass of clear water

schedule 15 criminal justice act 2003 2007 definitive sentencing guidelines

cyclical / *wall painting house of the cecii*

spring

yellow as a
chick my easter shorts
cut wire where her
beak pulped

winter

each night
the hammer breaks
my windows to make
tears fall on the
fresh snow

summer

the sheets
of fear hang clean
from my hands when
the wind blows they
dance

autumn

herbaceous borders
uncover wriggly roots day-mummy
driving the fork night-mummy
pressing my neck

a panther pounces at rams
running from her by a lake

black river

when the fingers came
at night your weeds rose up

when the rocks arrived
you rushed my brain's sluices

when the day returned
no hurt would surface

the stupendous task

at Herculaneum

can only be tentative and preliminary ; but

of the highest importance

ancient

Herculaneum must be excavated completely
for the good of the living

every year's delay makes
more difficult,

to carry out such work
claim the active support and co-operation of

the ideals   we   have in common.

my amah my armour

ah loh my baby bones are grown
though I have no photo of your face
to remember I still whisper
the words we made together

soo-soo for the potty
suck-suck my comforter
good-baby your hands patted

in singapore whenever mother
clawed the air with anger
you pooled calm water
bathed me in nurture

until aged one or two
in a paris corridor
I was pulled

                    away

                         from you
                         moon
                         of my baby night

                                        a carbonised cradle
                                        holding a baby's
                                        bones was missed

bains de mer

grown in an unconstrained bed
to navigate the veins of childhood
I cleanse in saltwater bonne maman

rattling dieppe's shingle
the tide carries back
our morning swims together

dew on spider webs
gates shawled in mist
the startled hydrangeas

eighty-four your robe zipped
sure-footed as a penguin
me your chick kept close

breasting the ice floe
lifted two breathing corks
in the churn of the channel

pistil: ovule:

has been well apart from german measles while   your
in france. difficult with medicines. aggressive &   tummy a
difficult with other children. bites and scratches. hardening
difficult to   ball of
get her off   ache
to sleep at
night. ie
spoiled++

stigma:

papa's photo shows you aged two waist-
deep in a field of french buttercups with your
red anorak zipped and the sky holding you

text of pistil derived from alice hiller's childhood medical notes

DESTRUCTION

impact   landscape

Here is Vesuvius,   green shady vines;

loved

hills   dances;

the home of Venus,

submerged in flames and

sad ash;   the gods   would not wish   such power.

st james's park in autumn

on the lake the double ducks
swim glued breast to breast

one is held under
the other rides on top

a cat pounces on a quail above
two ducks awaiting plucking

mosaic from the house of the faun

on the shoreline

> the violent
>   ground surge
>   followed
>   immediately
>   by a glowing avalanche,
>   came without warning
>   a shattered skeleton
>   blown off a terrace 60 feet
> above the marina a roman
>   soldier slammed face
>   down above sword
>   and scabbard
>   testifies to the force
> of the blast

papa there was no chronology for your illness   nothing was said when

you needed the stick   and then the wheelchair

you sent me drawings from the hospital   until your body became the house

through which death walked   but did not close the door

three small shrines found still upright

bonne maman the rosebuds
on the cup I sip your morning tea
from are faded by years of washing

astringent jasmine floats a lemon sun
up from your breakfast tray
even when the sky clouds over

and your bedroom mirror
flowers with salt garlands
foaming off the storm

phare d'ailly

papa the tide at vasterival was going out
when you were carried from our flat as I slept

your jaw swung
open like a latchless door

the sea is now 1km from
the site of pompeii

15

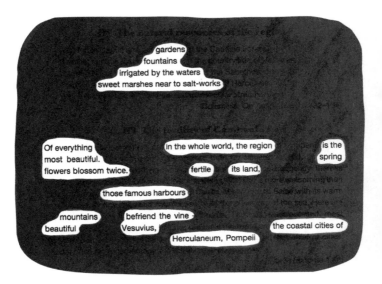

gardens
fountains
irrigated by the waters
sweet marshes near to salt-works

Of everything
most beautiful.
flowers blossom twice.

in the whole world, the region

is the
spring

fertile   its land,

those famous harbours

mountains
beautiful

befriend the vine -
Vesuvius,

the coastal cities of

Herculaneum, Pompeii

16

observed by two women
the female painter creates a
herm of priapus

wall painting removed from the house of the surgeon

I am just home from the hospital mother and this knot
is as red as a new tulip so you can easily break its neck

this knot is a rose sprinkled with itching
powder pricking between my legs

this knot is the coiled raisin danish that sticks to my fingers
when you buy two on saturdays for our treat

this knot is the sewing basket filled with my letters home
that one night you will put into the fire and burn

because this knot is lodged fast inside me
sometimes I eat and I eat until I hurt

this knot is a flashing red beacon telling everyone
I am what they can come and get

17

remnants / *silvae*

always the mountain top
threatens us with death

cold no sweater can shake
the swollen anus

who will believe when
these deserted places bloom again

a body remembers in
the only language available

our entombed cities
their absent peoples

italicised text from statius *silvae* 4.4.78–85

18

love me

show me how to crack
the shell against the rim
and open two jagged cups

slip the yolk
from lip to lip without
piercing its round

dip the whisk
to whip the clear
slop to foam

drop in flour
spoon by spoon
glossing the sauce

you know I love you

feeling the scorch
of the oven's mouth
sliding in with our prize

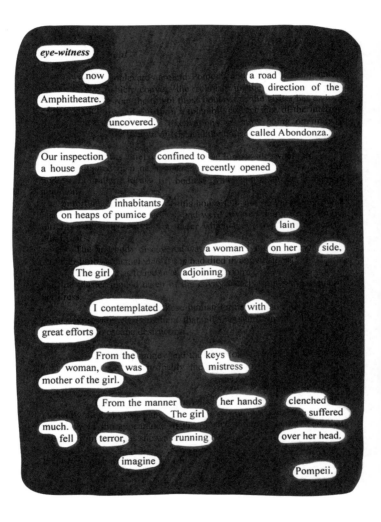

eye-witness

now   a road
                                    direction of the
Amphitheatre.

uncovered.

called Abondonza.

Our inspection   confined to
a house   recently opened

            inhabitants
on heaps of pumice

                                            lain

                    a woman   on her   side,

The girl   adjoining

I contemplated   with

great efforts

        From the   keys
    woman,   was   mistress
mother of the girl.

        From the manner   her hands   clenched
                        The girl   suffered
much.
    fell   terror,   running   over her head.

        imagine

                                            Pompeii.

in the vineyard

a hoer's mattock
slants abandoned
where the fugitives
fall face down
their arms cradling their heads

between the benches
of the triclinium veins
open along the stems
that trained them

and tunics ruck up
baring buttocks
to the slow pine
unfurling its
umbrella of death

snowfall

cold is over everything
people scoop and throw handfuls
the sun is slipping
down over the edge of the earth

cold has stolen all the colour
and stripped the trees
birds have nowhere to shelter
small ones fall off branches
and lie without moving

cold says
you are not loved
you are not wanted

I am the tower and the tower is my silence
I am the cold and the cold is all over

speak winter   inhabit me

it is small with a pavement of
mosaic, and fluted ionic columns
so white that it dazzles you

percy bysshe shelley on the temple of isis at pompeii 1818

eumachia accepts all tributes

mount the steps
aim your bright stream

this gold is collected by fullers
to dissolve grease and stains

slaves trample clothes
clean with their bare feet

no matter how they rinse
urine lingers within our tunics

let none of this enter you

child your closed lids
are the hulls
of my dreams
do not betray me

do not pee in your pants
to smell like your mother
or get into the bath
where she has peed already

I would rather the masts
of your boats put out my eyes
than see you there
between those white thighs
like her good girl

and now the ashes were falling
on the ships thicker and hotter
the closer they approached and
also pumice stones and cinders

pliny the younger on the eruption of vesuvius

after a visit to the doctor

because my tummy hurt
for my birthday mummy bought
a ballerina from harrods
with soft cake
under her frosted skirt

other times our treat
was ice cream bears
in chocolate coats
frozen flat on their backs

but then   when we set off
in the november rain to get
back our stolen mini

she made me leave the house
with no top on

and all our scary way
on that dark coach
my mac's slippity zip
shivered
against my bare skin

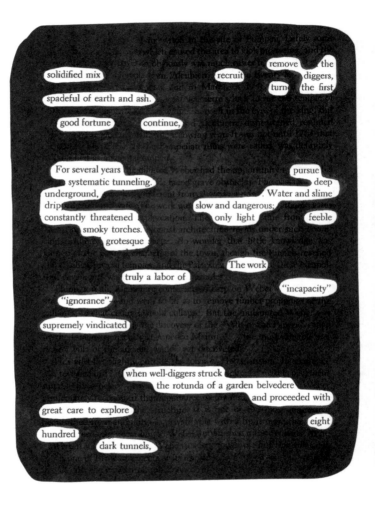

solidified mix   recruit   remove   the diggers,
                                          turn   the first
spadeful of earth and ash.

good fortune   continue,

For several years   pursue
        systematic tunneling.   deep
underground,   . Water and slime
drip   slow and dangerous;
constantly threatened   only light   from   feeble
        smoky torches.
        grotesque

                              The work

        truly a labor of

                                                            "incapacity"
"ignorance"

supremely vindicated

        when well-diggers struck
                the rotunda of a garden belvedere
                                        and proceeded with
great care to explore   eight
hundred
        dark tunnels,

terracotta figurines

queened by her gold sheath
and ferragamo shoes

the flame of her hair
eclaired into a marie-antoinette

in that narrow white room
where our two bodies touch

her freckled hands wield
secateurs with curved beaks

as she shows me how to strip
the leaves from cut flowers

then threads each one with wire
so its bloom cannot stop

a thracian in an unvisored helmet
faces a hoplomachus in a visored
helmet armed with shield and sword

primary or classical anorexia [1977]

in the dark

> *sparrow becomes*
> *clever and pretty*

feather by feather plucked

> *recovery is easier*
> *for fledglings*

some nights tore

> *starvation sows fine*
> *down over her body*

carried away made to keep still

> *tranquillisers improve*
> *eating and sleeping*

her clawed breast would regrow

> *psycho-sexual conflict*
> *is inadmissible and unseemly*

tessellation

from her bed in the white cloud alice watches the commode she uses
as a toilet   it is three steps away but cannot be mentioned   she has
not been allowed out of this room since she arrived   pills drop her
into nothing at night and hollow out her days

                                                      the doctor asks if alice
is feeling better   alice thinks about the menu cards they make her
fill   within the leather armchair the doctor's thighs spread warmed
marzipan   alice says she is getting used to being here

                                                            the doctor's
hair is pulled back into a bun   she suggests that after alice leaves
hospital she could travel to the desert and learn arabic   alice imagines
tents and camels and cushions with tiny mirrors

                                                        the doctor lights her
cheroot filling alice's lungs with heavy candy floss   the doctor says
you must understand you're not your mother   you can only get well if
you move far away from her

                                            as the doctor speaks   giant scissors
snip around the window   once these scissors have cut all the way
round the frame alice rises up light as a leaf   cold air is lifting her
out into the waiting sky

                          alice   both physically and mentally   is much
                          less depressed and more outgoing   I think she
                          is beginning

                          letter, alice hiller medical notes, 1 november, 1977

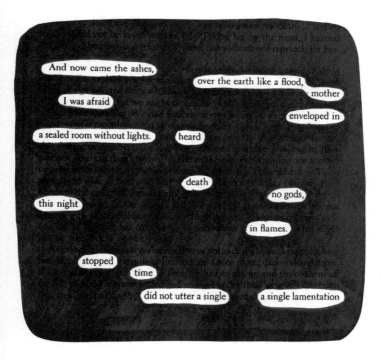

And now came the ashes,

over the earth like a flood,

mother

I was afraid

enveloped in

a sealed room without lights.   heard

death

no gods,

this night

in flames.

stopped

time

did not utter a single   a single lamentation

33

evidence / *fissure*

amphitheatres carved from
bone stagger into stone

show your raw part

traps in floors
troughs to drain blood

streak the lace-trimmed

bars protect watchers
from the creature

nightdress taken off

when attacked
leaves marks

in the laundering dark

as rain drunk
by growing grass

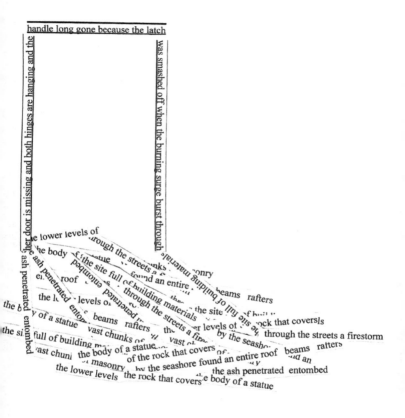

handle long gone because the latch

er door is missing and both hinges are hanging and the

was smashed off when the burning surge burst through

the lower levels of
the body of the statue
ash penetrated roof
entombed levels of beams rafters
the body of a statue vast chunks of
the site full of building the body of a statue
the lower levels the rock that covers the body of a statue
found an entire beams rafters
through the streets a firestorm
by the seashore through the streets a firestorm
the rock that covers
found an entire roof beams rafters
the ash penetrated entombed

bird of winter

how are you today   this morning I find a chaffinch
I hear you're eating   no chirrups come from its swollen beak
you're sleeping ok   the chaffinch's beak is almost as long as its body
have you enjoyed the books I brought in   the beak is reddish in colour
you're thirteen   you must grow up   although the chaffinch keeps
and separate from your mother   fluttering onto the curtain rail
you can't live at home   it is not strong enough to fly

tombs lined all the roads
leading to roman towns

the garden incorporates an
ornamental bird bath and a
domestic shrine

rue de l'aurore

on a gold-tasselled rope the
turquoise surface of bonne
maman's pendant
                    sways

        raising the wet sea
between my two palms then
turning me littler than my
own whisper

            and sailing me to
the island where papa is
waiting for us to sing

sonnez les matines
sonnez les matines

to the birds roosting
high in the ivory pines

circular

the ball is me
caught

                                  in lank
                             winter grass

slick as the hair
between the legs

                       in the bedroom
                which the round moon

peeks into
then looks away

                                  a bronze fish hook was
                             found in the house of the
                                      gladiators

proceeding blindly through tunnels and through narrow passages much will be broken much will be destroyed nor will it ever be possible to see the noble buildings in their entirety

scipio maffei on the excavations at herculaneum november 1747

seize your slave girl
whenever you want it's
your right

december 1976

I want to sleep curled
in the bottom of the freezer
where lost petits pois lie
like bullets among
the plucked pheasants

o let me be naked in clear plastic
and ice myself to a lolly
so nothing can fit inside me

mummy is decorating our tree
she tells me to thread stars
through its prickly branches
on christmas eve we set
angels above candles

we measure wine and cinnamon
then when the carol singers come
I pass round warmed mince pies
orbiting all her smart friends

we will rise early the next morning
when all the frost has melted
my worshipped body will be as heavy
as the grey sky above st katharine's
where we will kneel side by side
while the vicar says *our father*

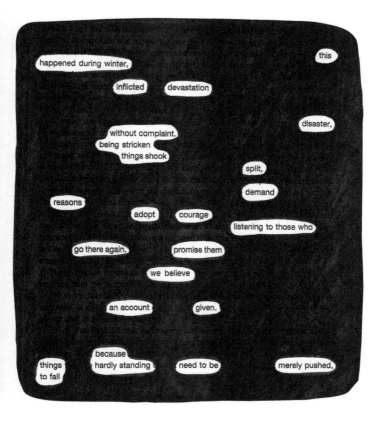

41

joujou

first time released
I unspooled

               then dropped

but her quick tug
wound my nub back up

reeling me in until
my string could not

slip and I climbed
unaided to the

the wrist
she flicked

in ancient rome joujous
were toys for girls

lace-making

after *la dentellière*

the young coiffeuse is frightened
she wants this but also she doesn't
the pick-up is sophisticated
she meets him over a lonely glace vanille
lingering on the breton seafront

tucked under your alpaca I watch
alongside you bonne maman
he kisses her into a folie
the young coiffeuse becomes
a fish in a pool of rods
caressed by rising bubbles

I feel them tickling you say
this is an important film
handing me long steel pins
to prick out my own pattern

later the coiffeuse is a lobster in a tank
with the doctor's tongs descending
knowing I was in a hospital like hers
you give me bobbins
wound with strong white cotton

then the lobsters are out on the floor tiles
and my hands begin lace-making
because we are inching side by side
out towards the turning windmills
the blue uncatchable waves

some beams that were burnt to a
coal and crumbled to pieces when
touched others not burnt and the
wood of these so hard and tough
that a knife would scarce cut

visitor to herculaneum 1752

                              the shape of her bosom
                       perfectly   preserved
                              when ash hardened

imprint of a young woman

we kissed all the way
home in the rain

the husk of your voice
musked my being

to enter your scented hair
rest my head on your belly

was to become a key
in the lock of the world

and open my whole
self to our turning

becoming your channel of pearl

I'm skipping school   mid-afternoon
o love let me dive down
deep where the water stills
to kiss each one of your unfolding selves

we freely share their oyster beds
our fresh new scents
within the frangipani lagoon
where we canoe through foam

my ghosts watch us from the shore palms
trying to cast out their hooked lines
when I finger your opened lips my sweet
I am reeled back   jerk by jerk
my skin stippling with fear

my skin stippling with fear
I am reeled back jerk by jerk
when I finger your opened lips   my sweet
trying to cast out *their* hooked lines

my ghosts watch us from the shore palms
where we canoe through foam
within the frangipani lagoon
our fresh new scents
we freely share   their oyster beds

to kiss each one of your unfolding selves
deep where the water stills
o love   let me dive down
I'm skipping school mid-afternoon
becoming *your* channel of pearl

valentine

a china heart
enamelled with violets

lies in a leather box
lined with silk

the heart shuts
with a golden clasp

on a doily
these words

I once belonged
to someone dear

note: this memory comes shagged with flies

I went down into the pit
conjectured to have been an
amphitheatre all were adorned
with grotesques

camillo paderni on visiting herculaneum 1740

elegy for an eight year old

she perches upright as a needle
before morning break

outside cold fog
is vanishing all the trees

there are fossils on the show and tell table
blue birds' eggs   clay pipes someone dug up

in the library iron fingers
are climbing out of the haunted book

their classroom is beginning to smell
of cabbage and mince

the girls will be skipping
in the playground soon

tiger masks with no
eyes frighten the wall

mr ward says she's moving
onto the green book for maths

underneath her wool tights
the hurt place stays on fire

every way
she shifts

bronze statues of five women
known as *the dancers* were
found in the villa dei papyri
with eyes of stone and ivory

uprising in blue and silver

my anger rings the anvil
which shoes the mare

where I was ridden
hooves crescent the sky

the holly tree

some nights the holly tree prickles me awake
its eyes are red berries pecked by birds

the holly tree claims my veins for its sap
the holly tree wants me of the chill clay

the holly tree says *follow the moon's path in bare feet*
the holly tree lays me a robin amongst brown leaves

in the grove my clothes are lifted
and my nectar is drunk

in the grove my body must
join the priestess   skin on skin

while we roll   and we wrestle
me so small   her so big

mirror

[above] first steam your face *a young girl in profile* use a clean tissue *gazing at something* what comes out *in her hands* will be brown or yellow *possibly a scroll* may turn infected

my bad fingers *her intensity of expression* pick and squeeze *has led some scholars to* skin rubbed with sandpaper *suggest that* afterwards *she was a figure* I can't look *drawn from life* telicately open ... silk threads attached to the edge

is ... less ... m e outgoing. I

the ink ... of iridesces

think she ... to appreciate life i ... all ... king close to

... thou it was

taking .... Getting caught ... too tired to

... previous ... gs we ... wrong ... find a way

... Rash on ... k ... fore.

reconstruct ... ut of th ... orion ... rphan fragments

... periods ... w if she can ...

the first ok ... orwards unroll

... a withdraw ... rl, ... ie. I did not

... an Alice told ...

... extracti

Tele one to s ... st. ... we ... 'blinded'

... tized f ... omnia.

carb ... isation ... highly fragile ...

... W ... long disc ... ion

... under-age ... ships. I.

complained of ... depression,

deep in ... infrared ray ... jum

helped ... hiatrist, a ... ave not ... I c ... not

relation ...

... fra ... us ... defied ... tempts

... her ten Dalm no, ... to come

back fo ... l. ve not seen her sin ...

... d not believe o. ...

... I find ... si ... ye

... oping with ... est of her abiliti ...

a fam race of l ...

... k lir ... a pale grey b ... round ... now it made sense

GLADIATORIAL SCHOOL   TRAINING

6 December   Continuing to clear the earth

columns painted red

20 December   in the building adjacent to the town walls.

were found shackles

with three cross-bars

irons

leaving spaces   between them.

a lock 10 inches high,

a rod

fastening the prisoners' legs   the

the hole

bolt   passed.

when they begin to have feathers

first by word then by touch
he adjusts her on the sofa

squabs are left in the nest
with their legs crushed

until she turns tender
to his wanting

with their mothers so
they can eat the food

when he drives her home
she stands unplugged

they feed themselves
and their chicks all day long

she fills her mouth
with bread with chocolate

qui iam pinnas incipiunt
habere relincunt in nido
inlisis cruribus et matribus
uberius ut cibo uti possint
obiciunt eo enim totum
diem se et pullos pascunt

varro *on agriculture* III vii 10–11

excavation of the gladiatorial barracks pompeii

in the pocket of my coat
a screw waits to rip

the tip of the finger
that dips in for change

but the screw is not real
you say with a laugh

I wipe off the blood

the whole room is painted,
though plainly and 4
skeletons were found there
perhaps of prisoners

report of discoveries 20 december 1766

dogfish sardines anchovies
octopus lobster conch and
a single kingfisher

mosaic house of the faun

sea level

there will always be the city
beneath this city charted by no one
where columns of stone tears
cling to the ceilings

whose people were once
lost or vaporised
their houses and temples
buried and forgotten

but let these people   who are my people
enter your lives again

and hope will shaft passages
up through the bedrock
until we swim free within
the breathing harbour of morning

libation

brussels was a grey cygnet the november morning I was driven home from school before break and mummy sat up straight on the sofa in her yellow swan beak dress to tell me my papa was dead but when she opened the bible picture book to read a story I could not hear her because wild wings were beating around my head.

             I am the shoots from papa's buried roots growing underground where no one can see me   crisp rabbits' ears driving out of darkness my white leaves sprout from his old stump   when I am awake I love chicory in french called endive   bitter cooked or raw and only harvested by torchlight I eat the food of the dead dressed with vinaigrette

i.m. 22 novembre 1972

the blue vase was found in
a tomb vines grow over its
surface supporting flowers
and songbirds

sagittae

l	l	l
ll	ll	ll
lll	lll	lll
llll	llll	llll
w e	w e	w e
peel	peel	peel
o f f	o f f	o f f
bark	bark	bark
llllll	llllll	llllll
wing	wing	wing
flight	flight	flight
llllllll	llllllll	llllllll
what	what	what
we're	we're	we're
held to	held to	held to
ground	ground	ground
against	against	against
blades our	blades our	blades our
arrowheads	arrowheads	arrowheads
llllllll	llllllll	llllllll
fired	fired	fired
we'll	we'll	we'll
leave	leave	leave
your	your	your
hold	hold	hold
llllll	llllll	llllll
e a t	e a t	e a t
a i r	a i r	a i r
llllll	llllll	llllll
take	take	take
each	each	each
cruel	cruel	cruel
mark	mark	mark
o u t	o u t	o u t
llllll	llllll	llllll
then	then	then
grow	grow	grow
o u r	o u r	o u r
split	split	split
body	body	body
back	back	back
into	into	into
tree	tree	tree
lllll	lllll	lllll

here victoria is unconquered

slide in with your stories
    these are easy pickings

tell her about the years down
under   the beatings in the children's
home you ran away from

and your *whore-mother* left back in britain
don't leave out the cruel priest-fathers

see how she's listening   yes
kiss the girl with the aubergine
hair and just-bought lipstick

                    don't worry if she's shaking

lead her upstairs in her black
t-shirt   her eyes are closed
pull back cold bedding

ease down her
leopard-skin leggings

when she's braced
mount
this young warhorse

she has chosen you
to ride her out

            towards a new freedom

graffito found on the wall of one of the private rooms of the lupanar

63

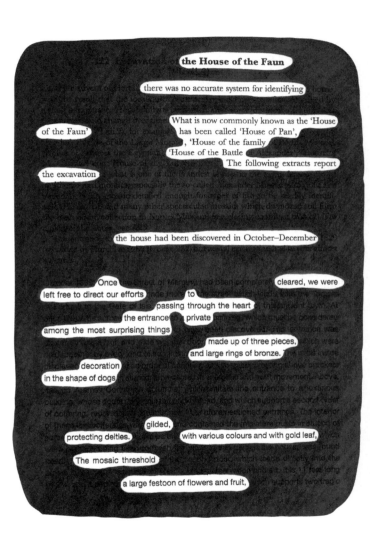

the House of the Faun

there was no accurate system for identifying

What is now commonly known as the 'House
of the Faun' has been called 'House of Pan',
, 'House of the family
'House of the Battle
The following extracts report

the excavation

the house had been discovered in October–December

Once cleared, we were
left free to direct our efforts to
passing through the heart
the entrance private
among the most surprising things
made up of three pieces,
and large rings of bronze.
decoration
in the shape of dogs
gilded,
protecting deities. with various colours and with gold leaf,
The mosaic threshold
a large festoon of flowers and fruit,

quadrant

silence:
like soft pink
kissings her own words
are spread onto the iced cakes
fed into the mouth
of the little girl

intimidation:
steel hooves thunder
along their corridor kick
hard in the kitchen then
rear up high in the
bedrooms

exclusion:
later lies puff out on
washing lines   because
she will not wear them the
young woman must
walk out naked

redemption:
open sky and water
wind-blink a clear pool
of june silver   rushing
her skin with spangled
rings of joy

vesuvius

blast apart your peak
shatter the rock straight up

surge black rivers from your veins
make bright night heavy day

pour down ash and pumice
muffle our streets with mourning

press your lips against
those who turn their faces

enter our towns
lean against our houses

until walls buckle
windows cry glass

shift this stifling stone
billow forth the wrecks we hold

scour out our hurt
let grief melt the ash

until vines climb your slopes again
until birdsong is heard

like an immense tree trunk
it was projected into the
air and opened out with
branches

pliny the younger

benediction / *holistic conservation*

dog I have loved bless my face with a small curl of your pink
tongue

i. *identify*

- *patterns of deterioration*
- *areas of reconstruction*
- *previous interventions*

I hold your foreleg inch of white fur shaved square

ii. *treat*

- *clean and consolidate surfaces*
- *fill cracks and voids*
- *re-adhere flaking paint*

time floats   lick me again

iii. *reintegrate*

- *minimally inpaint areas of loss and abrasion*
- *use neutral tones in lacunae to reinstate legibility*
- *do not attempt to reconstruct missing elements*

the fluid enters as harebells on the high downs

iv. *stabilise long-term*

- *protective sheltering*
- *environmental control measures*
- *monitoring*
- *regular maintenance*

where we bound through the dry grass forever

instructions for management of wall paintings

oiseaux d'hiver

pour mon père

we pushed two nets between water and sand
bellying out pelican beaks
to scoop the purple hair of the sea

I perched beside you on the cliff
watching the swan with smoke for a neck
lower our sun in its wake

you lay between hospital sheets
while I taught my pillow in the whispering dark
papa is dying like the fish we caught

each night that I was attacked
you floated farther from me
and when I cried for help
only the soil of your grave
answered my open mouth

now novembre sheds gold tears
on the bandstands and hooped railings
of our loved parks in paris

I track them past the swings
where you fledged my down into feathers
then along the verdigris river

until you rise visible
at last to me papa

your face no longer lost

but vivant
speaking
from the water

inside a scarlet room the female
daemon opens her blue wings and
raises her staff in blessing above a
half-naked woman

wall painting from the villa of the mysteries

mothered

field mouse seeking winter shelter   you nested in my right ovary

grew to the size of a curled hare

stoppered my shifting channels
with your swelling mass

poppies flowered from my vulva where they inserted their probe

I *breathed* then *held*
we were stalks of corn entered at night by car headlights

the nurse wrapped your bulge in a cotton shroud
I was slung dreaming onto their metal altar
the silver harrow opened from my ribs to my pubic bone

you stared out into your first and last daylight
in my hollowed tree you were yellow and grey autumn
even leaving
your mushroom gills held fast to their spores

spring forgot

was sung awake
by slow starved birds

six years now –
where you rooted
scars twist and hammock

among their opening leaves

                    I live

o goddess isis

make me your chick
feed me from your beak
twice a day rattle your sistrum
call me back from death

each spring reassemble
my scattered parts
beat me into the sky
on hawk wings

I will be your horus
hovering above them
as they shovel the ashes
from fluted columns

I will shake cymbals
clear of silence
bury pinecones
in the temple floor
raise beloved osiris

I will offer up my voice
until the ibis fly
free of the carvings

until the stars
of your nipples dissolve night
until the hems of your tunic
reveal the sunrise

Notes and acknowledgements

P.v 'in this place was found a bronze sistrum' cited 'E9, Excavation of the Temple of Isis' p.124 *Pompeii and Herculaneum: A Sourcebook*, Alison E. Cooley and M.G.L. Cooley, Routledge, 2014 – within a 1775–1776 excavation report of the Temple of Isis in Pompeii. Details used in 'o goddess isis' are also derived from this report.

P.4 'the needle's eye sews red silk'. Schedule 15 Criminal Justice Act 2003, 2007 Definitive Sentencing Guidelines.

P.7 'the stupendous task' **erasure** p.53 *Herculaneum, Past Present and Future*, Charles Waldenstein, Macmillan, London 1908.

P.10 text of 'pistil' derived from alice hiller's medical notes.

P.11 'destruction impact landscape' **erasure** from Martial, *Epigram* 4.44 translated by Alison E. Cooley and M.G.L Cooley, cited 'C25 The eruption's impact on the landscape' p.55 *Pompeii and Herculaneum: A Sourcebook* Alison E. Cooley and M.G.L. Cooley, Routledge, 2014.

P.13 'on the shoreline' italicised text from p. 20 *Herculaneum: Italy's Buried Treasure*, Joseph Jay Deiss. Copyright © 1966, 1985 by Joseph Jay Deiss; renewed © 1994 by Joseph Jay Deiss. Used by permission of HarperCollins Publishers.

P.16 'gardens fountains' **erasure** from Columella *On Agriculture*, 10.132–36, and Florus *Epitome* 1.16, both translated by Alison E. Cooley and M.G.L. Cooley cited 'H1 The natural resources of the region' and 'H2 The fertility of Campania' p. 229 *Pompeii and Herculaneum: A Sourcebook*, Alison E. Cooley and M.G.L. Cooley, Routledge, 2014.

P.18 italicised Latin text from Statius, *Silvae*, 4.4.81–85 abridged and loosely translated by alice hiller. Loeb Classical Library, Harvard University Press, Cambridge, Massachusetts, 2015.

P.20 'eye-witness' **erasure** *The Times*, Wednesday 17 June, 1863.

P.22 quote taken from letter by Percy Bysshe Shelley on visiting the Temple of Isis at Pompeii in 1818, cited pp.204–5 *The Complete Pompeii*, Joanne Berry, Thames and Hudson, 2013.

P.24 Plinius Gaius *Letters* Book VI, Letter 16 Macmillan, New York, 1915 cited p. 12 *Herculaneum: Italy's Buried Treasure*, Joseph Jay Deiss. Copyright © 1966, 1985 by Joseph Jay Deiss; renewed © 1994 by Joseph Jay Deiss. Used by permission of HarperCollins Publishers.

P.26 'remove the solidified mix' **erasure** from p. 28 *Herculaneum: Italy's Buried Treasure* Joseph Jay Deiss. Copyright © 1966, 1985 by Joseph Jay Deiss; renewed © 1994 by Joseph Jay Deiss. Used by permission of HarperCollins Publishers.

P.32 Letter from medical practitioner in alice hiller's medical notes.

P.33 'and now came the ashes' **erasure** Plinius Gaius *Letters* Book VI, Letter 20 Macmillan, New York 1915 cited p.14 *Herculaneum: Italy's Buried Treasure*, Joseph Jay Deiss. Copyright © 1966, 1985 by Joseph Jay Deiss; renewed © 1994 by Joseph Jay Deiss. Used by permission of HarperCollins Publishers.

P.35 'her door is missing' concrete poem : rubble of words in the doorway taken from phrases describing the eruption on pp. 35–6 *Herculaneum: Past and Future*. Andrew Wallace-Hadrill, Frances Lincoln Ltd, London, 2011, published in collaboration with The Packard Humanities Institute, Los Altos, California.

P.39 Scipio Maffei, on the excavations at Herculaneum november 1747, cited pp.33–4, *Rediscovering Antiquity: Karl Weber and the Excavation of Herculaneum, Pompeii and Stabiae*, Christopher Charles Parslow, Cambridge University Press, 2011.

P.41 'this happened during winter' Seneca the Younger, *Natural Questions*, translated by Alison E. Cooley and M.G.L. Cooley, cited 'C1, A contemporary account of a major earthquake', p.39 *Pompeii and Herculaneum: A Sourcebook*, Alison E. Cooley and M.G.L. Cooley, Routledge, 2014.

P.43 *La Dentellière* [1977], or *The Lacemaker*, directed by Claude Goretta and starring Isabelle Huppert and Yves Beneyton based on the 1974 novel *La Dentellière* by Pascal Lainé.

P.44 J Northall, *Travels in Italy, containing new and curious observations on that country*, London 1766, p.257. Cited p 129 *Rediscovering Antiquity: Karl Weber and the Excavation of Herculaneum, Pompeii and Stabiae*, Christopher Charles Parslow, Cambridge University Press, 2011.

P.45 'imprint of a young woman' citation "the shape of her bosom [...] perfectly preserved when ash [...] hardened" abbreviated from a description of the excavation in 1771 at the Villa of Diomedes where the skeleton of a young girl was found within her imprint left in the ash.

P.48 Camillo Paderni, to the Royal Society of London, 1747, cited p. 33 *Rediscovering Antiquity: Karl Weber and the Excavation of Herculaneum, Pompeii and Stabiae*, Christopher Charles Parslow, Cambridge University Press, 2011.

P.52 'mirror' The italicised text is taken from a caption of a wall painting of a young girl examining something – text on p.102, reproduction of wall painting on p.103 of *The Complete Pompeii*, Joanne Berry, Thames and Hudson 2013.

P.53 'delicately open' combines text from '*Reading a Herculaneum Scroll: Source University of Kentucky*, citing Dr Brent Seales, available online, and *Unlocking the scrolls of Herculaneum*, Robin Banerji, BBC News Magazine 20 December 2013 available online, with phrases from alice hiller's teenage medical notes.

P.54 'gladiatorial training school' **erasure** text taken from 1766 excavation report cited 'D48 The excavation of the Gladitorial Barracks' p.85 *Pompeii and Herculaneum: A Sourcebook*, Alison E. Cooley and M.G.L. Cooley, Routledge, 2014.

P.55 Marcus Terentius Varro, *On Agriculture*, III. vii 10–11, Latin p. 466, *Cato and Varro on Agriculture*, Loeb Classical Library, Cambridge, Massachusetts and London, England, 1935. Italicised translation within poem by alice hiller.

P.56 'excavation of the gladitorial barracks pompeii' citation taken from 1766 excavation report cited 'D 48 The excavation of the Gladitorial Barracks', p.85 *Pompeii and Herculaneum: A Sourcebook*, Alison E. Cooley and M.G.L. Cooley, Routledge, 2014.

P.63 'here victoria is unconquered' Translation of graffito found on the walls of the Lupanar [*CIL* IV 226] or brothel and cited on p.111 of *The Complete Pompeii*, Joanne Berry, Thames and Hudson, 2013.

P.64 'the house of the faun' **erasure** text taken from analysis by Alison E. Cooley and M.G.L. Cooley followed by Fiorelli's account of the discovery in 1830 of the House of the Faun cited 'A22 Excavation of the House of the Faun' p.17 *Pompeii and Herculaneum: A Sourcebook*, Alison E. Cooley and M.G.L. Cooley, Routledge, 2014.

P.66 'like an immense tree trunk it was projected into the air, and opened out with branches', Pliny the Younger, Plinius Gaius *Letters* Book VI Letter 16 Macmillan, New York 1915 cited p.12 *Herculaneum: Italy's Buried Treasure*, Joseph Jay Deiss. Copyright © 1966, 1985 by Joseph Jay Deiss; renewed © 1994 by Joseph Jay Deiss. Used by permission of HarperCollins Publishers.

P.67 details of the processes of 'holistic conservation' of wall paintings taken from the practices of the Getty Conservation

Institute and the Herculaneum Conservation Project described on pp. 148–9 *Herculaneum and the House of the Bicentenary: History and Heritage*, Sarah Court and Leslie Rainer, The Getty Conservation Institute, Los Angeles, 2020.

Versions of some of these poems have previously appeared in *The Cambridge Literary Review, tentacular, Chemistry,* 2018 Creative Futures Literary Awards, and *Midnight Listening,* Arvon, 2018.

Living beyond sexual abuse

Some readers of *bird of winter* will, like me, have been groomed and sexually abused as children or teenagers. My own childhood and adolescent experiences traumatised and shamed me deeply. I was only able to seek professional help in my thirties. In my fifties, I still need support from time to time. Some people with our history make contact with support sources younger. Others wait many decades.

Whatever our ages, many of us find it valuable to work with someone with specialised training. It can help us understand that we were not complicit in what was done to us as children and teenagers, and that we should not feel of less worth for having been subjected to a crime which we had no means of resisting. Reaching these understandings, in a kind and respectful context, can also make it possible to live more freely and joyously again. I have written about claiming life in the aftermath of sexual abuse in childhood on my blog, alicehiller.info

For people seeking help, one route is to speak with your doctor. In addition, the UK charity Mind gives organisations supporting people making their lives in the aftermath of sexual abuse. I have listed some below. More details can be found on the Mind website.

Help for Adult Victims of Child Abuse   havoca.org

Lifecentre lifecentre.uk.com 0808 802 0808 (freephone) 07717 989 022 (textline)

The National Association for People Abused in Childhood 0808 801 0331   napac.org.uk

One in Four 0800 170 0314   oneinfour.org.uk

The Survivors Trust 08088 010 818   thesurvivorstrust.org

To excavate my own history of being groomed, and then sexually abused as a child, and along with the adolescent aftermath, was not easy. However deep the dark, we turn instinctively towards the light. Writing these poems, the shadow worlds of Pompeii and Herculaneum were a source of intense illumination for me.

Having only studied Latin to GCSE, I am indebted to the Classicists whose scholarship I cite here. Alison E. Cooley and M. G. L. Cooley's *Pompeii and Herculaneum: A Sourcebook* is a rich collection of classical texts, excavation reports, and original materials from the two cities. I am very grateful for their generous permission to cite from this essential work.

Herculaneum by Joseph Jay Deiss gives the reader the opportunity to imagine walking around the ancient city and its subsequent excavations.

Many of the poems responding to physical objects arose from the illustrations of wall paintings and historical finds in Joanne Berry's *The Complete Pompeii*. I am very grateful for her kind permission to quote her caption text in 'mirror'.

Andrew Wallace-Hadrill's sumptuous photographic record and analysis, *Herculaneum Past and Future*, is an invaluable, immersive experience. He generously allowed me to create a rubble of phrases from his text in 'her door is missing'.

Sarah Court's and Leslie Rainer's *Herculaneum and the House of the Bicentenary* gives a key sense of how past and present fit together, and what a contemporary restoration entails. I thank them both for allowing me to respond to their account of conserving wall paintings in 'benediction/ holistic conservation'.

bird of winter would not have taken flight without the support of a community of writers. First among them is Pascale Petit, who mentored me under the Jerwood Arvon scheme, and gave me the example of her life and work. I am also indebted to Rebecca Tamás and Karen McCarthy-Woolf for reading some of these poems in draft with keen eyes, and to Natalie Whittaker for looking over the final manuscript. As friends, Isabelle Baafi, Neil Douglas, Rowan Hisayo Buchan, Julie Irigaray, L.Kiew, Natalie Linh Bolderston, Anita Pati and Karen Smith have embodied kindness and encouragement. The poets of the Covent Garden Stanza co-generate a powerhouse of radical energies. My Jerwood Arvon sisterhood of Romalyn Ante, Seraphima Kennedy and Yvonne Reddick show what it is to stand as one. Kaveh Akvah, Nuar Alsadir, Vahni Capildeo, Mary Jean Chan, Sasha Dugdale, Linda Gregerson, Wayne Holloway Smith, Sarah Howe, Rachel Long, Kathryn Maris, Sandeep Parmar and Shivanee Ramlochan have been lights along the way.

In closing my deepest gratitude goes to the brilliant, extraordinary Deryn Rees-Jones, who asked me to become a Pavilion poet, and created the collection's structure. Alison Welsby and Zeenia Naqvee at LUP, with Alistair Hodge, have been ceaselessly diligent and supportive in hatching the manuscript into a book.

On the home front, my sons Ze and Pendragon Stuart, together with Jacqueline Ullmann, and my husband Julian Maddison, have been rock solid at all times. I could not have written *bird of winter* without them.

bird of winter is dedicated to the memories of Ah Loh, George François Hiller, Alice Prud'hon Hiller, Concha Celorrio, and Falcon Stuart. Their love allowed me to dispel the darkness amidst which my life began. 'o goddess isis' is for Falcon.